Renewed

Healing the Mind Through the Word of God

ROSE METHENY

Cover and interior design by Brandi Lariscy-Avant

Published by Grace and Glow Press | Phoenix, Arizona

www.rosemetheny.com

First Edition: July 2025

ISBN 979-8-9992180-3-2

This book is a work of nonfiction. Some names and identifying details may have been changed to protect the privacy of individuals. All stories are shared from the author's personal experience and testimony.

For bulk orders, speaking inquiries, or book clubs:
hello@rosemetheny.com

DEDICATION

To the One who never left me—Jesus, this is for You.
You saw me at my lowest and still called me Yours.
You stepped into the battlefield of my mind,
held me through every breakdown,
and gently rewired every thought with truth.
You are my Healer, my Counselor, my Prince of Peace.
Thank You for renewing me—again and again.
This book is my offering of worship.

To Larry—my rock.
You have loved every healing version of me.
Your steady presence, your prayers, your grace…
have been a gift I never knew I needed.
Thank you for always pointing me back to Jesus.

To my son, Chris—my reason for wanting more.
You gave me the courage to heal,
to grow, to break generational chains.
This journey started for me…
but I kept going for you.

And to every woman who's ever felt like her thoughts were too loud,
her past too painful, or her mind too far gone—
this is for you too.
You are not crazy.
You are not alone.
You are being made new.

With all my love,
Rose

CONTENTS

FOREWORD

This book isn't just a testimony—it's an invitation.

An invitation to be honest about what's really going on inside your mind. To take off the mask. To exhale. To let the Word of God speak to the parts of you that no one else sees.

If you've ever felt overwhelmed by your thoughts… If you've ever questioned your sanity, your identity, your worth… If you've ever smiled in public while silently breaking inside…

You are not alone.

I know that place intimately. I lived in that mental war zone for years —confused, fragmented, and exhausted from fighting battles no one could see.

But then something changed.

Not because I tried harder. Not because I finally figured it all out. But because Jesus met me in the wreckage of my mind and began to heal me through His Word.

The healing wasn't overnight. It was quiet. Gentle. Steady. One truth at a time.

This book is the story of that healing. It's a journey through lies, identity confusion, and trauma—but it's also a journey into freedom, clarity, and peace.

Renewed isn't about perfection. It's about process. It's about returning to the feet of Jesus again and again and letting His truth untangle what the enemy tried to bind.

If you're holding this book, I believe God led you here. And I pray with every page, you begin to experience the same transformation I did— not because of me, but because of Him.

May this book lead you deeper into His Word. May it remind you that your mind is not too far gone. And may you discover what I did—that Jesus can restore every broken thought, every hidden hurt, and every piece of you that you thought was lost.

You are not alone. You are being renewed.

With love and expectancy,
Rose

INTRODUCTION

Hey beautiful one,

Before we dive in, I just want to say—*I'm so glad you're here.*

Whether someone recommended this book, you stumbled across it in a moment of searching, or you felt God whisper to your heart to pick it up… you're not here by accident.

Renewed is the follow-up to my first book, *Redeemed: A Journey from Brokenness to Freedom.* If *Redeemed* was written for the heart—*Renewed* is written for the mind. Because healing doesn't stop at salvation. Sometimes, it begins there.

This book is personal. It's tender. It's full of truth, tears, and the kind of healing that only Jesus can bring. It's not just a book—it's an invitation. A safe space to be honest about what's been going on in your thoughts, your patterns, and your inner world.

I pray as you read, you'll feel the presence of God wrapping around you like a warm blanket. I pray the lies lose their power, the shame begins to lift, and the truth starts to feel louder than your fears.

Take your time. Pause when you need to. Grab your Bible, a journal, maybe a cozy drink, and let the Word of God speak to every part of you—especially the parts no one else sees.

You're not too far gone. You're being renewed—one whisper, one verse, one moment at a time.

Let's walk this journey together.

With so much love,
Rose

The Battle in the Mind

Romans 12:2 (NIV) *"Do not conform to the pattern of this world, but be transformed by the renewing of your mind."*

I didn't always know I was in a war. Not the kind with guns or armies. But a quieter, deadlier kind—one that lived inside my head.

The battleground was my mind, and for years, I didn't know that the thoughts I was thinking weren't actually me. They were the echoes of trauma, fear, shame, and lies—things that had taken root long ago and twisted the way I saw myself, God, and the world around me.

There were days when I couldn't think straight. Nights when I couldn't sleep. Mornings when I'd look in the mirror and see a stranger—angry, overwhelmed, broken. And yet somehow, I lived through it.

But I wasn't whole. I wasn't well. And deep down, I knew it.

What I didn't know was that the brokenness in my mind wasn't a sign that I was crazy—it was a sign that I needed healing. Real healing. The kind only Jesus could give.

No one told me that unhealed trauma could split your mind into pieces. That you could walk through life carrying different versions of yourself, each one trying to protect you in a different way. I just thought something was deeply wrong with me.

And maybe that's where the enemy had me most—believing I was too messed up, too damaged, too fractured to ever be normal… let alone renewed.

But the truth? God never asked me to be normal. He just asked me to be His.

He saw the chaos in my thoughts. He saw the fragments in my soul. And He called me beloved.

This chapter of my life—the one you're about to walk through—wasn't clean or polished. It was painful, messy, confusing… and holy.

Because in that mess, Jesus didn't just visit me—He rescued me. He didn't just silence the noise—He renewed my mind.

He came into the war zone of my thoughts, and with every truth, every whisper, every tear-soaked scripture, He began rebuilding what had been broken for so long.

This is the story of how I went from mentally tormented to mentally restored. From confused to clear. From fragmented… to whole.

Not because I figured it out. But because grace found me in the ruins—and Jesus stayed.

PAUSE & REFLECT

Chapter One—The Battle in the Mind

Colossians 3:2 (NIV) *"Set your minds on things above, not on earthly things."*

Reflection Questions

Have you ever felt like your mind was at war? What did it sound like inside your head during that time?

What thoughts or patterns have tried to define you that you know aren't from God?

What does a "renewed mind" look or feel like to you right now?

Prayer

Jesus, You see every thought I think and every battle I face. You know how tired I've been—how loud the lies can get. Thank You for never leaving me, even in the darkest corners of my mind. I invite You into my thoughts, my memories, and my mental habits. Begin Your healing work in me, Lord. Renew my mind with Your truth. Anchor me in peace. Fill me with clarity and remind me who I am in You.

Amen.

Two

Lies That Linger

John 8:32 *"You will know the truth, and the truth will set you free."* (NIV)
Proverbs 23:7 (NIV) *"For as he thinks in his heart, so is he."*

Long before I understood what trauma was… Long before I knew how to fight back with the truth of God's Word… I believed lies.

Not because I wanted to. But because they were the only voices I heard.

Lies whispered in childhood. Lies screamed through silence. Lies that wrapped around my identity like chains. "You're too much." "You're not enough." "You're damaged." "You'll never be whole." "You'll never be free." "You'll always be broken."

Those lies became my inner soundtrack. And the more I believed them, the more they shaped me. Until I didn't know where the lies ended and I began.

There were times when I felt like I wasn't just one person. I had formed different versions of myself… almost like separate personalities. And they weren't imaginary. They were real to me. Characters. Protectors. Each one carried a piece of the pain I didn't know how to process. Each one helped me survive when I didn't feel safe in my own skin.

The Mean Old Man

Loud. Angry. Critical. He barked in my mind like a drill sergeant, always telling me I was never good enough. He hated weakness. He hated softness. He expected perfection and punished anything less. He didn't smile. He didn't comfort. He didn't care. But in a strange way, he made me feel like I had control—because he was always "in charge." He was my defense against chaos. If I could beat myself up before anyone else did, maybe it wouldn't hurt as much. He was cold, calculated, and sharp-edged. But cold doesn't feel. And I didn't want to feel.

The Strong Black Woman

Bold. Fearless. Unshakable. She didn't flinch. She didn't cry. She didn't need anyone. She showed up when I needed a warrior—when I felt exposed, weak, or small. She took up space on purpose. She walked into rooms like she owned them. She was fierce, elegant, and always in control. She had fire in her eyes and a don't-you-dare energy that made me feel safe when the world felt threatening. She wasn't just strong— she commanded strength. And when I felt powerless, she took the wheel and dared anyone to try her.

The Scared Little Girl

Timid. Tearful. Afraid. She lived in the shadows, barely speaking above a whisper. She tiptoed through life, always waiting for the next explosion, the next rejection, the next abandonment. She cried herself to sleep more nights than anyone knew. She didn't trust the world—but she longed to be held by it. She carried my innocence, my confusion, and the weight of a thousand unanswered questions. She was fragile… but deeply precious. And though she was often overlooked, she was the part of me that most desperately wanted love.

The Ghetto Black Man

I called him "The Ghetto Black Man." Not to stereotype—but because that's exactly how he showed up in my mind. He was quick, smart, and streetwise. He was tough. He could read a room in seconds, clock everyone's energy, and anticipate danger before it even had a name. He trusted no one and stayed ready for war—emotionally, mentally, physically. But he wasn't just tough—he was hilarious. Witty. Loud. Sarcastic. The kind of funny that cut through fear like a knife. He cracked jokes in tense rooms. He made people laugh when there was nothing to laugh about. He made *me* laugh—when I didn't even know I needed it. He knew how to talk his way out of anything, stand his ground, and never show weakness. He was my street-smart protector and my comic relief. He wasn't gentle—but he was brilliant. And sometimes, he made me laugh just enough… to keep breathing.

The Sexy Woman

Confident. Magnetic. In control. She walked in heels with her head high and a don't-mess-with-me aura that could silence a room. She knew how to turn heads, steal attention, and use charm like currency. She never begged. She never chased. She kept her distance while making everyone come closer. But underneath her glossy surface… was a deep ache. She wore her sexuality like armor, not connection. She seduced to survive, not to feel loved. She looked free—but she was just as bound. Her power wasn't rooted in worth… it was rooted in fear. But she was still a part of me. And she, too, longed to be seen—not for her body, but for her heart.

None of these versions of me were fake. They were real responses to real pain. I didn't make them up—I made them out of survival. They were born from silence, fear, and childhood wounds that never got the chance to heal.

And for years, I thought they were me. But they weren't. They were masks. They were broken pieces of a shattered soul.

And here's the miracle… Jesus didn't tell me to choose just one and pretend the rest didn't exist. He didn't say, "Get it together." He didn't flinch. He came for all of me. Every fragment. Every false identity. Every role I played just to stay alive.

And piece by piece…He brought me back together.

He whispered to every part: "You are Mine." "You are safe now." "You can rest."

Jesus didn't shame the versions of me that tried to survive. He just gently led them back to truth.

To my truth. To His truth.

That I am loved. That I am not crazy. That I am His.

And the more truth I received… The more the lies began to unravel.

I need to pause here and tell you the truth: I was scared to share this part. Not because it's not real—but because it's *so* real, and I know how people can be. I've wrestled with the fear that if I shared how fractured my mind felt at times—how these different versions of me helped me survive—people would label me. Call me crazy. Question my stability. Use it against me.

But here's what I've learned: **what the world might call "crazy," Jesus calls "wounded."** And He doesn't reject the wounded. He heals them. These parts of me weren't imagined. They weren't attention-seeking. They were my body, my mind, my spirit doing what they had to do to make it through trauma I never should have had to face.

And if you're reading this and silently nodding… if you've ever felt "split," scattered, unsafe in your own thoughts—*this part is for you too.* You are not alone. And you are deeply, dearly loved by a God who wants to restore every single part of you.

Identity Matrix: The Parts That Helped Me Survive
Throughout Chapter 2, I introduced different "versions" of myself—identities I formed to survive pain I didn't yet know how to process. None of them were fake. Each one held a piece of the story. For anyone who related or resonated, I created this simple matrix to recap the roles and responses I carried:

IDENTITY	DESCRIPTION
The Strong Black Woman	Bold. Fierce. Protected me with power.
The Ghetto Black Man	Hilarious, tough, streetwise. Made me laugh to keep me breathing.
The Mean Old Man	Harsh, critical, expected perfection.
The Scared Little Girl	Fragile, fearful, longed to be loved.
The Sexy Woman	Magnetic, armored, deeply aching.

This isn't a checklist—it's a reflection. Maybe you've carried your own cast of protectors. Maybe this helps you name them too.

You are layered, complex, beautifully human. And Jesus is not overwhelmed by any part of you.

PAUSE & REFLECT

Chapter 2—Lies That Linger

2 Corinthians 10:4 (NIV) *"The weapons we fight with are not the weapons of the world. On the contrary, they have divine power to demolish strongholds."*

Reflection Questions

What lies have followed you for most of your life? Where do you think they came from?

Which version of "you" have you leaned on the most to survive?

What would it feel like to allow Jesus to speak truth to that version of you?

Prayer

Lord, You know every part of me—even the parts I've hidden or the ones I created to protect myself. Thank You for not turning away from my brokenness. Thank You for loving me in every form I've ever shown up in. I lay down every mask and every false identity at Your feet. I ask You to speak truth where lies once lived. Heal the places in me that were shaped by fear and restore me with Your love. I trust You, Jesus. I trust You with every part of me. Amen.

Three

The Breakdown Before the Breakthrough

Psalm 34:18 (NIV) *"The Lord is close to the brokenhearted and saves those who are crushed in spirit."*

One night, I was lying on the floor of my room, completely undone. I had cried until I couldn't breathe. I whispered through clenched teeth and broken sobs, "I can't do this anymore. Something is wrong with me." And I meant it. Every word.

But healing didn't come through me trying harder. It came through me surrendering completely.

Jesus didn't fix me that night. He found me. And He didn't find the best version of me—He found the shattered, exhausted, terrified one. And instead of pulling away… He sat with me. In the silence. In the ache. In the fog.

I didn't get up healed. I got up held.

That was the beginning of everything. From that moment forward, healing came in waves. It wasn't instant. It was holy and slow and real.

For the first ten years of my walk with Jesus, I cried. Every church service. Every worship song. Every time the Word was preached. Tears would pour down my face before I could even explain why.

I didn't know it at the time but the tears were healing me. Cleansing me. Setting me free.

I'll never forget my very first women's retreat. I didn't know a soul. I came alone, feeling small and invisible.

During the first chapel service, they invited us to come to the altar to pray. So I went. I knelt down… and in the quiet of my heart, I made a simple request to God: "Lord, please send me a best friend. Whoever comes and prays for me—let her be the one."

I stayed kneeling for what felt like forever. Tears streamed down my face. People passed by… but no one came to pray for me. Not one person.

I remember whispering through the tears, "Lord, You didn't send anyone."

And in the stillness of that moment, He answered so clearly: "I did send someone. I sent My Son."

I'll never forget that. Because in that moment, Jesus reminded me that even when no one else shows up—He does. He didn't just want to give me a friend. He wanted to be the Friend who would never leave. The One who would always come close. The One who sees me. Chooses me. Stays with me.

I couldn't believe God actually loved me. The real me. The fractured me. The messy, insecure, ashamed, scared little girl inside.

And because I couldn't believe it… I wept. Not out of sadness, but out of release. My soul was finally exhaling.

Every tear felt like a piece of shame falling off. Every cry was a cleansing. Every sob was a surrender.

Jesus was washing me with His love. He was healing memories I hadn't yet remembered. He was freeing me from chains I didn't even know were wrapped around my mind. He was setting me free.

What I once thought was the end of me…Was really the beginning of a whole new me.

Because God does His most powerful work in the places we fall apart. And He didn't leave me there—He rebuilt me.

PAUSE & REFLECT

Chapter 3—The Breakdown Before the Breakthrough

Psalm 147:3 (NIV) *"He heals the brokenhearted and binds up their wounds."*

Reflection Questions

Have you ever experienced a season where your mind or emotions felt completely broken? What did that look like or feel like for you?

Can you identify a moment when God met you in your pain—not to fix you, but just to hold you?

What emotions have you been holding back that might be part of your healing journey?

What would it look like to surrender—not strive—for healing?

_____

_____

_____

_____

_____

Prayer

Jesus, I've spent so long trying to hold it all together. I've worn masks, stuffed emotions, and fought battles in my mind that no one else could see. But You've seen every moment of it. You were there in my breakdowns. You heard every whispered prayer through my tears. Thank You for being the kind of Savior who doesn't walk away when things get messy. Thank You for holding me when I couldn't hold myself. I surrender to Your healing work. I give You permission to touch the places in me that still hurt, to bring peace where there has been torment, and to rebuild what's been shattered. I trust You. I'm not too far gone. I am Yours.

Amen.

Truth That Shatters Chains

John 8:32 (NIV) *"Then you will know the truth, and the truth will set you free."*

Truth didn't come to me like a lightning bolt. It came like a whisper. Quiet… steady… relentless.

For so long, my mind had been a swirl of lies deep, embedded beliefs that felt like facts. I didn't even question them. I just lived by them.

"You're too broken." "You're not wanted." "You're too much." "You're not enough."

"You're stupid." "If they knew the real you, they'd leave."

Those lies had names. Faces. Stories. They were attached to memories, experiences, and years of unhealed pain. But when I started walking with Jesus—really walking with Him—I slowly started to see that not everything I thought was true.

The Bible wasn't just a book anymore—it became my mirror. And for the first time, I began to see who I really was.

Chosen. Loved. Forgiven. Set apart. Safe. Seen.

It didn't happen all at once. It happened one truth at a time. One verse at a time. One moment in His presence at a time.

I would read Scripture and start to weep—not because I was sad, but because I was seen. Every time I opened the Word, it felt like God was speaking directly to my trauma, to my thoughts, to the lies that had kept me in chains for so long.

It was as if Jesus was saying, "Let's go back to where that lie was born. Let Me replace it with something true."

And He did.

I remember reading Isaiah 43:1: "Do not fear, for I have redeemed you; I have called you by name; you are Mine." That "you are Mine" hit different. It crushed something in me—in a good way. The orphan spirit. The abandoned girl. The broken pieces. They were being claimed. Covered. Healed.

That's the thing about truth: it doesn't just inform you. It transforms you. It doesn't just set you free from what others have said about you— It sets you free from what you've said about yourself.

Jesus wasn't just renewing my mind with nice words—He was retraining my brain to think in alignment with heaven.

One of the first people who ever encouraged me to sit still with the Word was my husband, Larry. Early in our marriage, he gently told me, "Babe, I think you need to spend more time with Jesus. You need to sit at His feet."

I had never heard that before. *Sit at His feet?* I looked at Larry and said, "What does that even mean?"

He said, "Go into a room. No distractions. Just you, your Bible, and some worship. Let God love you through His Word."

And that's exactly what I did. I didn't always know what I was doing— but I showed up. And day by day, those moments became sacred. I wasn't just reading Scripture—I was *receiving* it. I was learning to let God love me back to life… one verse at a time.

I remember one of the first verses the Lord gave me was **Psalm 27:13**: *"I remain confident of this: I will see the goodness of the Lord in the land of the living."*

At the time, I didn't feel like I was seeing any goodness. My mind was still a mess. My heart still hurt. But I clung to that verse like a lifeline. And now, looking back, I realize—I was already beginning to see it. Because that verse wasn't just a promise… it was a seed. And sitting at Jesus' feet was how it started to grow.

Instead of reacting from fear, I started responding from love. Instead of assuming rejection, I began expecting favor. Instead of walking in shame, I learned to walk in sonship. (Daughtership? Lol. But you get me.)

It wasn't perfect. Sometimes the lies tried to come back—familiar voices that tried to pull me under again. But now I had a weapon. Truth.

I learned to speak it out loud. To write it down. To declare it in prayer. Even when I didn't feel it—especially when I didn't feel it.

Because that's how chains break. That's how strongholds fall. Not with feelings—but with truth.

I remember one day, I was on my way to speak at a women's event—to share my testimony, to talk about what God had done. I was praying in the car, just me and Jesus. And I whispered, "Lord, let them see me the way You do."

And in the stillness, He spoke something I'll never forget.

"My daughter… I want you to see yourself the way I see you."

I froze. Tears welled up in my eyes. Because in that moment, I realized… I was still struggling to believe it. Even as I was getting up to share my story—there were still parts of me that hadn't fully received His truth. Parts of me that were still unsure. Still ashamed. Still hiding.

It's hard to explain... but it was like Jesus was gently holding up a mirror —not to expose me, but to free me.

That's the thing about renewal. It's not a one-time moment. It's a lifetime of letting His truth replace our fear. A daily surrender. A constant returning to the voice of the One who knows us fully—and loves us still.

PAUSE & REFLECT

Chapter 4—Truth That Shatters Chains

Romans 12:2 (NIV) *"Do not be conformed to this world, but be transformed by the renewing of your mind."*

Reflection Questions

What lies have you believed about yourself—maybe for so long that they've started to feel like truth?

Can you recall a time when God spoke something into your heart that shattered a long-held lie? What did that feel like?

What truth from God's Word do you need to start declaring over your life—out loud and often?

Where do you still need to invite the truth of Jesus to rewrite the narrative?

Prayer

Jesus, I've believed so many things that were never from You. Some of them were whispered in childhood... others shouted in pain... and some, I've repeated to myself over and over. But today, I lay those lies down. Replace every false belief with Your truth. Speak life into the parts of me that still feel ashamed, unseen, or unworthy. Help me see myself the way You see me—redeemed, chosen, and deeply loved. Let Your Word become louder than my wounds. Let Your voice be the one I follow. And let Your truth be the chain-breaking, heart-healing anthem of my mind from this day forward. In Your name, Jesus, amen.

Five

The Power of a Sound Mind

2 Timothy 1:7 (NKJV) *"For God has not given us a spirit of fear, but of power and of love and of a sound mind."*

I didn't know I could ask God for a sound mind. I thought I was just supposed to manage it. Fight to stay sane. Push through the fog. Keep smiling so no one would know how broken I was inside.

But 2 Timothy 1:7 wasn't just a feel-good verse. It was my promise. God didn't give me fear. He gave me power. He gave me love. And He gave me a sound mind.

The first time I read that verse and really let it sink in, I remember saying out loud, "Wait… You mean I don't have to live in mental torment anymore?" Because for years, I thought my broken mind was just something I had to accept. A cross to bear. A burden I'd carry forever. But that's not what my Father said.

He said I had access to a sound mind. A peaceful mind. A stable mind. A mind that wasn't spinning out with fear or shame or panic. A mind that could breathe. A mind that was whole.

It didn't come all at once. Healing came in layers—deep, holy, intentional. God didn't just snap His fingers and wipe away all the chaos.

He taught me how to walk it out. How to partner with Him. How to renew my thoughts daily.

And slowly, I began to experience what it felt like to think clearly. To sleep peacefully. To pray with confidence. To trust my own thoughts without second-guessing myself every five minutes.

That, to me, is the power of a sound mind: Not perfection. But peace. Not that the enemy stops trying—But that I no longer believe him when he speaks.

I still have moments. I still have triggers. But now I know what to do with them. Now I know what's mine… and what's a lie. Now I know that I am not at the mercy of my emotions or my past. I am held. I am safe. And I have been given a sound mind.

PAUSE & REFLECT

Chapter 5—The Power of a Sound Mind

2 Timothy 1:7 (NKJV) *"For God has not given us a spirit of fear, but of power and of love and of a sound mind."*

Reflection Questions
Have you ever believed that your mental or emotional struggles were just something you had to live with forever? Where do you think that belief came from?

What does a "sound mind" look like for you personally? What would peace in your thoughts actually feel like?

Are there any thoughts or thought patterns you need to surrender to God right now so He can begin healing and renewing them?

Prayer:

Jesus, thank You for the promise of a sound mind. Not just temporary relief, but real, lasting peace. Thank You that I don't have to live in fear, anxiety, or confusion anymore. Thank You for reminding me that healing is possible, that wholeness is possible, and that freedom is my inheritance. I surrender my thoughts to You—every racing worry, every lie I've believed, every place in my mind that feels unstable. Come in, Lord. Fill those spaces with truth. Train my mind to trust You. Guard my thoughts with Your peace. Let me walk in the strength, love, and soundness that only comes from You. In Jesus' name, amen.

$\mathcal{Six}$

The Healing of Memories

Psalm 23:3 (NIV) *"He restores my soul…"*

I used to think healing meant forgetting. Stuff it down. Move on. Pretend it never happened. But Jesus doesn't heal by erasing our memories —He heals by entering them.

There were moments from my past I didn't want to touch. Scenes I had buried so deep I forgot they existed—until they started showing up in my emotions, my triggers, my reactions. I didn't want to go back. But Jesus did.

Because He loved me too much to leave those parts of me untouched.

Sometimes healing looks like a memory rising up out of nowhere. Sometimes it looks like crying during worship and not knowing why. Sometimes it looks like shaking as your body remembers something your mind has tried to forget. And in those moments, the enemy tries to shame us: "You're not healed. Look at you—still a mess."

But Jesus says something different: "Let Me into this memory. Let Me walk you through it. Let Me show you where I was, and what I want to redeem."

I remember one day in prayer, a memory surfaced that I hadn't thought of in years. It was painful, blurry, and familiar all at once.

And before I could panic or shut it down, I felt the Lord so clearly: "I'm with you in this. Let's walk through it together."

It was scary. But it was also freeing. Because for the first time, I wasn't alone in that memory. Jesus was there.

I saw Him there in places I had only remembered feeling abandoned. I saw Him protecting me, weeping with me, covering me—even in the worst moments of my past. And somehow, knowing He had been there all along... healed something in me.

He didn't take away the memory—He took away the sting. He removed the shame. He silenced the lie that I was alone or unprotected. He rewrote the narrative with truth.

Healing of memories is sacred work. It's not easy. It's not fast. But it's holy.

Because Jesus doesn't just want to give us a new future—He wants to redeem our past.

And when He enters those broken, buried places... Even the most painful memories can become altars of healing.

PAUSE & REFLECT

Chapter 6—The Healing of Memories

Isaiah 43:18–19 (NIV) *"Forget the former things; do not dwell on the past. See, I am doing a new thing!"* (Note: "Forget" here means not to live stuck in the past—but to move forward, healed and free.)

Reflection Questions

Are there memories from your past that still feel painful, confusing, or "off-limits"?

What emotions surface when those memories rise up? Can you name them without shame?

Can you imagine inviting Jesus into one of those memories? What do you think He might want to show you or speak over you?

What would it mean for you to believe that even your past can be redeemed?

_____

_____

_____

_____

_____

Prayer

Jesus, there are places in my past that still ache—places I've buried, avoided, or tried to forget. But You see them. You were there for every moment I thought I was alone. You never left me, not even once. Today, I invite You into those memories. Walk with me through the pain. Show me where You were. Speak truth where lies have lived for too long. Heal what still hurts. Rewrite the story with Your love and restore what was stolen. I trust You to redeem even this. Thank You for being the God who doesn't waste anything—not even my broken past. Amen.

Seven

Worship as Warfare

Exodus 14:14 (NIV) *"The Lord will fight for you; you need only to be still."*

Psalm 32:7 (NIV) *"You are my hiding place; you will protect me from trouble and surround me with songs of deliverance."*

For most of my life, I didn't know I was in a war. And when I finally realized I was, I didn't know how to fight. But worship taught me.

I used to think worship was just the slow part of the church service—the emotional songs that gave you goosebumps and made you cry. And yes, sometimes it was emotional. Sometimes I did cry (okay—I always cried). But worship wasn't just an experience. It became a strategy.

Because there were days I couldn't pray. Days I didn't have the words. Days I was too mentally foggy, too heavy, too tormented to even think straight.

But I could worship.

I could turn on a song and sit in His presence. I could raise my hands with tears running down my face. I could whisper "Jesus, I trust You" even if my thoughts were a mess.

And every time I did… something broke.

Worship became my weapon. It silenced the noise. It shifted the atmosphere. It reminded my spirit that even if I couldn't control the storm around me—I could choose to praise in the middle of it.

There were mornings when I'd wake up already anxious—before my feet even hit the floor. So I started fighting differently. I'd blast worship music while getting ready. I'd sing through the fear. I'd speak truth over myself through the lyrics. Even if I didn't feel anything yet—my soul was learning to lead instead of follow.

Worship reminded me that I wasn't powerless. It pulled me out of myself and re-centered me on Him. It wasn't about sounding pretty— it was about taking territory.

And let me tell you—some of my deepest healing didn't come in counseling, or church, or even in prayer. It came in worship. In my bedroom. In my car. In the quiet places where it was just me, Jesus, and the sound of freedom rising.

Worship didn't erase my pain. It just reminded me I wasn't alone in it. And the more I worshipped, the more my mind started to align with heaven. The lies got quieter. The fear got smaller. And the truth got louder.

Because worship doesn't just move you—it moves the heart of God. And when He moves? Chains break. Darkness flees. And peace floods in.

PAUSE & REFLECT

Chapter 7—Worship as Warfare

Isaiah 61:1–3 (NIV) *"The Spirit of the Sovereign Lord is on me… to comfort all who mourn… and provide for those who grieve… a garment of praise instead of a spirit of despair."*

Reflection Questions

When has worship helped you get through something you didn't think you could survive?

What happens inside you—emotionally or spiritually—when you worship, even if you're not "feeling it"?

Are there places in your life right now where you need to stop striving and start worshipping? What would that look like practically?

How can you begin using worship as a weapon—something you run to instead of something you wait for?

_____

_____

_____

_____

_____

Prayer

Father, thank You for the gift of worship. Thank You that I don't have to fight my battles alone. Even when I don't have the words, You give me a song. Even when I feel weak, You surround me with Your presence. Lord, teach me to worship not just in joy—but in pain, in fear, and in the middle of the storm. Let worship rise from my spirit as a weapon of truth and victory. Silence the enemy's lies with every note I sing and every breath I offer You. Dwell in my praise, Jesus. Reign over my atmosphere. And let freedom flood in every time I choose to lift Your name. Amen.

Eight

Replacing Rumination
with Revelation

Isaiah 26:3 (NLT) *"You will keep in perfect peace all who trust in You, all whose thoughts are fixed on You."*

Rumination was my specialty. I could replay a conversation a hundred times. Rehearse what I should've said. Overanalyze every look, every tone, every silence. If something went wrong, I would sit in it—turn it over and over in my mind until I was exhausted.

I called it processing. But it wasn't healing me. It was tormenting me.

That's the thing about ruminating—it pretends to be productive. It disguises itself as "thinking things through," but really it's just worry with a better outfit.

And it left me stuck.

I couldn't move forward because my mind was always circling the past —what they said, what I did, what I didn't do, how I messed up, how I wish I could fix it.

It never ended. Until God showed me there was a better way.

He wasn't asking me to shut my brain off. He was asking me to invite Him into it.

Revelation is different than rumination. Rumination is me trying to figure things out. Revelation is God showing me something I never would've seen on my own.

And let me tell you—when I started replacing rumination with revelation, everything shifted.

Instead of spiraling in self-criticism, I started asking: "Holy Spirit, what are You saying right now?" "What's the truth in this situation?" "What do You want me to see, that I'm not seeing yet?"

And He answered.

Sometimes with peace. Sometimes with Scripture. Sometimes with a gentle correction. But always—always—with love.

I learned that every time I started spiraling, I had a choice. I could keep turning the same anxious thought over in my head… Or I could turn it over to Him.

That's how peace comes. That's how clarity comes. Not from control—but from connection.

God doesn't want to shut your mind down. He wants to renew it.

And the more I asked Him for His voice in place of my own overthinking, the more I found myself resting instead of rehearsing. Trusting instead of obsessing. Receiving instead of ruminating.

And let me tell you: There's nothing like the peace that comes when your thoughts finally align with truth.

PAUSE & REFLECT

Chapter 8—Replacing Rumination with Revelation

Philippians 4:6–7 (CSB) *"Do not worry about anything, but in everything, through prayer and petition with thanksgiving, present your requests to God. And the peace of God… will guard your hearts and minds in Christ Jesus."*

Reflection Questions

What's a thought or memory that you tend to replay over and over? What does it cost you emotionally or spiritually?

How do you normally respond when your thoughts start to spiral—do you try to fix them, stuff them, or feed them?

What would it look like to stop rehearsing and start asking God for revelation instead?

What truth or Scripture can you start declaring when rumination tries to take over?

Prayer

Lord, You know how easy it is for my mind to race—to fixate, over-think, and hold onto things that You never asked me to carry. I don't want to live in the cycle of mental chaos anymore. I want peace. Real peace. So I invite You into my thoughts. Interrupt every spiral with Your voice. Teach me to recognize when I'm rehearsing fear instead of receiving truth. Help me trade rumination for revelation—my anxiety for Your wisdom. And when I start to overthink again, gently pull me back to You. You are the calm in my mind, the stillness in my soul, and the One I trust to lead me into truth. Amen.

Nine

Learning to Think Like a Daughter

Romans 8:15 (NIV) *"The Spirit you received does not make you slaves, so that you live in fear again; rather, the Spirit you received brought about your adoption to sonship. And by Him we cry, 'Abba, Father.'"*

I spent most of my life thinking like a survivor. Always on edge. Always assuming the worst. Even when things were good, I was waiting for the bottom to drop out.

I wasn't trying to be negative. I just didn't know what it felt like to be safe.

I knew how to hustle. I knew how to overperform. I knew how to read people, adjust my tone, smile through the ache, and make everyone else comfortable—even if I was falling apart inside.

But you know what I didn't know how to do?

Receive love. Feel chosen. Think like a daughter.

I didn't realize how deeply the orphan mindset had shaped me. I didn't believe anyone was coming to rescue me—so I became my own rescuer.

I didn't trust love to stay—so I clung, chased, or pushed it away first. I believed I had to earn what God had already given.

Even after I got saved, I still struggled to see God as Father. I loved Him. I worshipped Him. But I was still bracing myself for disappointment, punishment, rejection.

Then one day, I heard someone say this: "Orphans beg. Daughters receive."

It undid me.

Because I had been begging. Begging for love. Begging for peace. Begging for worth.

But I already had it. I just didn't know how to receive it.

Learning to think like a daughter changed everything. It meant trusting that I was already accepted—not earning it day by day. It meant speaking to God not like a distant ruler, but like a loving Father. It meant walking into rooms without shrinking back, because I knew I belonged.

It didn't mean I was perfect. But it meant I was positioned.

I was no longer fighting for love... I was living from it.

God had already called me His. I just needed to start believing it.

Every time I felt fear rise up, I'd say, "I am a daughter." Every time I was tempted to hustle for approval, I'd whisper, "I am already loved." Every time I felt like I didn't belong, I'd breathe in the truth: "I've been adopted by the King."

Because thinking like a daughter isn't about pretending everything's okay. It's about knowing you're okay—even when everything isn't. Because your identity is rooted in something deeper than circumstance. It's rooted in Sonship.

And daughters walk differently.

PAUSE & REFLECT

Chapter 9—Learning to Think Like a Daughter

"See what great love the Father has lavished on us, that we should be called children of God! And that is what we are!" — 1 John 3:1 (NIV)

Reflection Questions

Do you find it easier to think like a servant or survivor than a daughter? Why do you think that is?

What lies about your worth or identity still try to sneak in and steal your peace?

When was the last time you really let yourself receive—without guilt, earning, or apology?

What would change in your life if you fully believed you are already loved, already chosen, and already safe?

Prayer

Father, I've spent so much of my life striving—trying to earn love, prove myself, or stay one step ahead of rejection. But today I choose to lay all of that down. I want to think like a daughter. Not an orphan.

Not a beggar. Not a survivor. A daughter. One who is already accepted, already treasured, already secure in Your arms. Teach me to walk in the confidence of being Yours. Heal every part of me that still feels unworthy or unsure. Let me rest in Your love, trust in Your goodness, and receive all that You've freely given me. I belong to You. Amen.

Ten

A New Way to See Everything

2 Corinthians 5:17 (NIV) *"Therefore, if anyone is in Christ, the new creation has come: The old has gone, the new is here!"*

There was a time when I saw everything through the lens of trauma. I saw people as unsafe. I saw myself as broken. I saw life as something to survive, not enjoy.

Even after I gave my heart to Jesus, I didn't realize how much of my vision was still fogged by fear, shame, and old patterns. Healing was happening—but so was something else: He was changing the way I saw.

One by one, the lenses started to fall off. The ones shaped by pain. The ones shaped by rejection. The ones shaped by my own self-hatred.

God was doing more than restoring my sanity—He was restoring my perspective.

I started seeing people differently. The ones who hurt me? I no longer saw them as giants. The ones who didn't protect me? I saw their humanity. And the people I used to envy or avoid? I saw them through eyes of compassion.

I started seeing myself differently too. Not through the lens of failure or shame—but through grace. I stopped analyzing every flaw and started noticing the fingerprints of God all over my life.

Even the hard parts. Even the chapters I never wanted to live—let alone tell.

Because when you've been healed, you don't erase the past. You just stop letting it define you.

I began to see that what was meant to destroy me had actually deepened me. That the tears I cried watered something sacred. That the healing I thought was just for me... was always meant for others too.

God didn't just redeem my story. He reframed it.

Now when I look back, I don't just see pain. I see purpose. I see patterns of grace. I see the hand of a Father who never left, even when I couldn't feel Him.

And now, I see the future differently too.

I don't wake up afraid anymore. I don't live waiting for the next breakdown or betrayal. I live expecting goodness. I live covered in peace. I live as a woman who's been renewed.

Not perfect. Not finished. But fully loved. Fully known. And finally—finally—free.

PAUSE & REFLECT

Chapter 10—A New Way to See Everything

Genesis 50:20 (NIV) *"You intended to harm me, but God intended it for good to accomplish what is now being done, the saving of many lives."*

Reflection Questions

How has your perspective changed since the beginning of your healing journey? What do you see differently now?

Are there parts of your story that once brought you shame but now reveal God's goodness?

In what areas are you still asking God to help you see with His eyes instead of your own?

What do you feel God is inviting you to believe about your future?

_____

_____

_____

_____

_____

Prayer

Father, thank You for healing not just my heart—but my vision. Thank You for lifting the fog, for peeling back the lies, and helping me see myself, my past, and my future through the lens of grace. You are so kind. Even the parts of my life I thought were ruined—you are using them for redemption. Give me eyes to see like You do. Let me walk into the future with clarity, confidence, and peace, knowing that I'm not who I used to be. I am a new creation. I am Yours. And I trust You with the rest of the story. Amen.

FINAL REFLECTION

I love church. I really do. I'm there when the doors open. I love worship. I love Bible study. I love gathering with my sisters and feeling the presence of God in community.

But I need to say this as clearly as I can: **it was only through reading the Bible—God's holy Word—that my heart began to change.**

Worship encouraged me. Church strengthened me. Community surrounded me.

But it was the *Word of God* that renewed my mind.

There is *nothing* like opening your Bible and letting God speak directly to your soul.

That's where the healing started. That's where the lies began to unravel. That's where I met Jesus again and again—not just as my Savior, but as my Shepherd, my Counselor, my Truth-Teller, my Friend.

If you want to change your life, read His Word. It's not just ink on pages—it's the breath of God, alive and speaking. And it will change you. Just like it changed me.

SCRIPTURES FOR CONTINUED RENEWAL

Here are some of the verses that helped me rewrite the soundtrack in my mind. May they do the same for you:

Romans 12:2 *Do not conform to the pattern of this world, but be transformed by the renewing of your mind. Then you will be able to test and approve what God's will is—his good, pleasing and perfect will.*

Colossians 3:2 *Set your minds on things above, not on earthly things.*

John 8:32 *Then you will know the truth, and the truth will set you free.*

Proverbs 23:7 *For as he thinks in his heart, so is he. "Eat and drink!" he says to you, But his heart is not with you.*

2 Corinthians 10:4 *The weapons we fight with are not the weapons of the world. On the contrary, they have divine power to demolish strongholds.*

Psalm 34:18 *The Lord is close to the brokenhearted and saves those who are crushed in spirit.*

Psalm 147:3 *He heals the brokenhearted and binds up their wounds.*

Isaiah 43:1 *But now, this is what the Lord says—he who created you, Jacob, he who formed you, Israel: "Do not fear, for I have redeemed you; I have summoned you by name; you are mine."*

Psalm 27:13 *I remain confident of this: I will see the goodness of the Lord in the land of the living.*

2 Timothy 1:7 *For the Spirit God gave us does not make us timid, but gives us power, love and self-discipline.*

Psalm 23:3 *He refreshes my soul. He guides me along the right paths for his name's sake.*

Isaiah 43:18–19 *Forget the former things; do not dwell on the past. See, I am doing a new thing! Now it springs up; do you not perceive it? I am making a way in the wilderness and streams in the wasteland.*

Exodus 14:14 *The Lord will fight for you; you need only to be still.*

Psalm 32:7 *You are my hiding place; you will protect me from trouble and surround me with songs of deliverance.*

Isaiah 61:1–3 *The Spirit of the Sovereign Lord is on me, because the Lord has anointed me to proclaim good news to the poor. He has sent me to bind up the brokenhearted, to proclaim freedom for the captives and release from darkness for the prisoners, to proclaim the year of the Lord's favor and the day of vengeance of our God, to comfort all who mourn, and provide for those who grieve in Zion—to bestow on them a crown of beauty instead of ashes, the oil of joy instead of mourning, and a garment of praise instead of a spirit of despair. They will be called oaks of righteousness, a planting of the Lord for the display of his splendor.*

Isaiah 26:3 *You will keep in perfect peace those whose minds are steadfast, because they trust in you.*

Philippians 4:6–7 *Do not be anxious about anything, but in every situation, by prayer and petition, with thanksgiving, present your requests to God. And the peace of God, which transcends all understanding, will guard your hearts and your minds in Christ Jesus.*

Romans 8:15 *The Spirit you received does not make you slaves, so that you live in fear again; rather, the Spirit you received brought about your adoption to sonship. And by him we cry, "Abba, Father."*

1 John 3:1 *See what great love the Father has lavished on us, that we should be called children of God! And that is what we are! The reason the world does not know us is that it did not know him.*

2 Corinthians 5:17 *Therefore, if anyone is in Christ, the new creation has come: The old has gone, the new is here!*

Genesis 50:20 *You intended to harm me, but God intended it for good to accomplish what is now being done, the saving of many lives.*

Closing Prayer

Jesus, thank You. Thank You for meeting me in the places I thought were too dark, too broken, or too far gone. Thank You for showing me that healing is possible, and that I don't have to live in torment anymore. You've walked with me through the wilderness, through the war in my mind, and into the wide-open space of freedom.

I surrender my thoughts to You daily, not because I'm afraid of breaking again—but because I trust You to keep rebuilding. Thank You for renewing me—heart, mind, and soul. Thank You for teaching me to think like a daughter, not a prisoner.

And for the one reading this now—may they know You the way I've come to know You: as Savior, as Healer, as the One who never gave up on them.

Let this book be more than a testimony. Let it be an altar. A place where You meet them, hold them, and make all things new.

In Your holy name I pray, amen.

THE JOURNEY CONTINUES...

Sis, you made it.

Page by page, layer by layer, you've walked through the renewing of your mind. Not by striving—but by surrender. Not by perfection—but by presence. Jesus met you here, and He's not done.

If something in these pages stirred your heart or spoke to your pain, I want you to know—this is just the beginning.

Keep showing up. Keep opening your Bible. Keep letting God speak to the parts of you that still feel messy or misunderstood.

You are not who you used to be.

You are becoming who He created you to be.

So walk in it, sis. Walk in peace. Walk in truth. Walk in power. Walk in freedom.

And when the lies try to creep back in… when your thoughts try to spiral… when the enemy whispers that you'll never change—

Open this book. Open your Bible.

And remind your mind: I've been renewed. I'm cheering for you. I'm praying for you. And I can't wait to see what God does with your story next.

With all my heart,
Rose

Stay Connected

Want more encouragement, updates, and resources on your healing journey?

Visit **rosemetheny.com**

- *Blog posts, book updates, and more from Rose*
- Join the email list for devotionals, freebies, and behind-the-scenes.
- Explore the full *Redeemed* and *Renewed* collection. Let's keep walking in freedom—together.

You can also reach out directly at:
hello@rosemetheny.com

www.ingramcontent.com/pod-product-compliance
Lightning Source LLC
Chambersburg PA
CBHW051648120626
46551CB00015B/2264